It's not will~power I need... it's won't power!

EXLEY

First published in Great Britain in 1983 by Exley Publications Ltd, 16 Chalk Hill, Watford, Herts WD1 4BN
Printed in Hungary by Kossuth Printing House

British Library Cataloguing in Publication Data
Wilson, Tom, *1931 –*
It's not willpower I need . . . it's won't power: Ziggy.
I. Title
741.5'973 NC1429.W5793

ISBN 0-905521-78-1 ISBN 0 905521 96 X (paperback)

ZIGGY™ is syndicated internationally by Universal Press Syndicate

...i NEVER MET A
CHOCOLATE CREAM BICCY
i DIDN'T LIKE !!

EVEN THO' I'M ON A DIET
I BUY A DOUBLE SCOOP
..BECAUSE I ALWAYS
DROP ONE !!

ICE
CREAM

I'M ON A SEA FOOD DIET ... WHEN I SEE FOOD, I EAT IT !!

I'M A VERY LIGHT EATER ...WHEN IT STARTS GETTING LIGHT... I START EATING !!

PEOPLE WITH WEIGHT PROBLEMS ARE ADVISED AGAINST ORDERING THE CHEF'S SURPRISE, SIR.
TOM WILSON

...WHEN IT'S TIME FOR DESSERT
NO ONE HAS TO ASK ME TWICE

...A WORD TO THE WIDE
IS SUFFICIENT

Tom Wilson

...I'M AFRAID TO LOOK DOWN...

...I'M DOWN TO ONE CUP A DAY !!

183 CALORIES
172 CALORIES
65 CALORIES
97 CALORIES
127 CALORI
24 CALORIES
42 CALORIE
86 CALORIE

ACTUALLY, i'M NOT eVeN HUNGRY ...i JUST HAVe A VeRY LOW SALeS ReSiSTANCe !!
MENU

i ALWAYS SEEM TO HAVE TROUBLE GETTING SERVED IN RESTAURANTS..
...MAYBE IT'S BECAUSE i ALWAYS LOOK LIKE i'VE ALREADY EATEN !
Tom Wilson

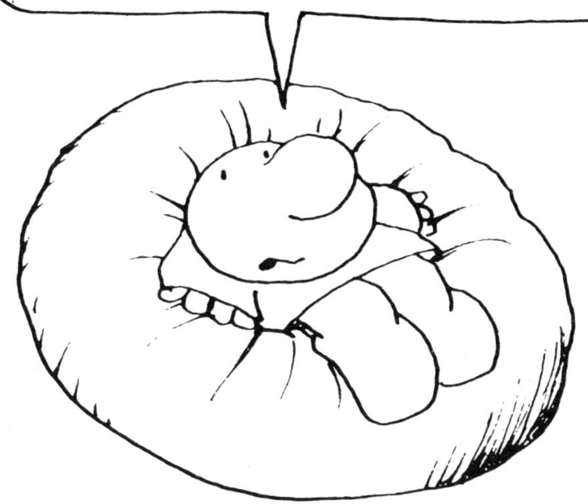
...AN OVERSTUFFED CHAIR IS ANY CHAIR I HAPPEN TO SIT IN!...
Tom Wilson

YOU ARE AN EXTREMELY CLEVER, TALENTED AND CHARMING PERSON, YOUR GOOD LOOKS ARE MATCHED ONLY BY YOUR SLIM PHYSIQUE! AND MARVELOUS PERSONALITY! ...YOUR FUTURE IS LUCKY, HEALTHY, AND BRIGHT! BUT WATCH OUT FOR FLATTERY, FALSE PROMISES AND SCHEMES AIMED AT TAKING YOUR MONEY...AND DON'T BELIEVE EVERYTHING YOU READ.
YOUR WEIGHT AND FORTUNE
20p

ABOUT THE ONLY TIME LOSING IS MORE FUN THAN WINNING ... IS WHEN YOU'RE FIGHTING TEMPTATION!!

DIETING IS A LOSING BATTLE

...IN FACT I SURRENDERED 3 YEARS AGO !!

...AS FAR AS I KNOW, THERE'S NO SUCH THING AS A DIET CREAM PUFF !!
tom wilson

GRROWL

BOY...I REALLY COULD GO FOR A MUSHROOM-SAUSAGE PIZZA !!

UH OH...I'M ALMOST BROKE !!

MMMM...THE FIRST POUND I EVER EARNED

MAMA MIA'
PIZZ
.. SENTIMENTALITY WILL LOSE OUT TO A MUSHROOM-SAUSAGE PIZZA EVERY TIME!

THIS SOFT DRINK HAS
NO SUGAR CONTENT
NO FOOD VALUE
NO CALORIES
NO ADDITIVES
NO REDEEMING SOCIAL VALUE
AND IS OF
NO EARTHLY USE TO THE
BODY WHATSOEVER

...NOW WE DON'T RECOMMEND THAT LAST EXERCISE FOR ANY BEGINNERS WHO'VE JUST TUNED IN !!

THIS PRODUCT CONTAINS
NO NATURAL INGREDIENTS,
NO CALORIES, AND NO MINERALS,
... BUT AT LEAST IT ISN'T
HARMFUL TO YOUR HEALTH!

SNACK-LETS
Diet Cola
for Santa
-Love, ZIGGY

IT'S A GREAT DAY FOR A WALK
.... THE KIND OF DAY THAT MAKES YOU GLAD TO BE ALIVE !!

THE END IS NIGH

THE WORLD ENDS TOMORROW

REPENT BEFORE IT'S TOO LATE

IT'S LATER THAN YOU THINK

..ONE DOUBLE HOT FUDGE SUNDAE WITH EVERYTHING
..AND HURRY !!
Tom Wilson

I REALLY SHOULD JOIN AN ATHLETIC CLUB OR SOMETHING...
...IF IT WASN'T FOR WRESTLING WITH MY CONSCIENCE.. I'D GET NO EXERCISE AT ALL !!

ACCEPT NO SUBSTITUTES
INSIST ON GENUINE
"PSEUDO"
SIMULATED ARTIFICIAL IMITATION FAD FOOD
TOM WILSON

THIS FILM UNRATED
...NO ONE WAS PERMITTED
SMOKERS
WED. THRU SUN.
FINAL WEEKS

NON·SMOKERS
NOW SHOWING
PART
BUBBLE GUM POPPERS AND POPCORN MUNCHERS
POP CORN

MOM'S RES
EAT ALL YOUR VEGETABLE OR YOU GET NO DESSERT!

BIG PHIL'S MOTOR CAFE
BIG PHIL DOESN'T LIKE IT WHEN YOU DON'T EAT EVERYTHING ON YOUR PLATE !!

MAMA MIA'S PIZZA
EAT IN OR PIG OUT
...IF THE LORD HAD MEANT US TO BE THIN, HE WOULDN'T HAVE CREATED PIZZA
12-30 Tom Wilson

ONE OF MY PROBLEMS IS
WHEN I GET DEPRESSED
ABOUT BEING OVERWEIGHT,
...I DROWN MY SORROWS
IN A CUP OF HOT CHOCOLATE,
AND A BOX OF CHOCOLATE
BICCIES!!

INGREDIENTS
MONOSODIUM GLUTAMATE, SODIUM GLYCERATE, RIBOFLAVIN(B_2), GLYCOL,

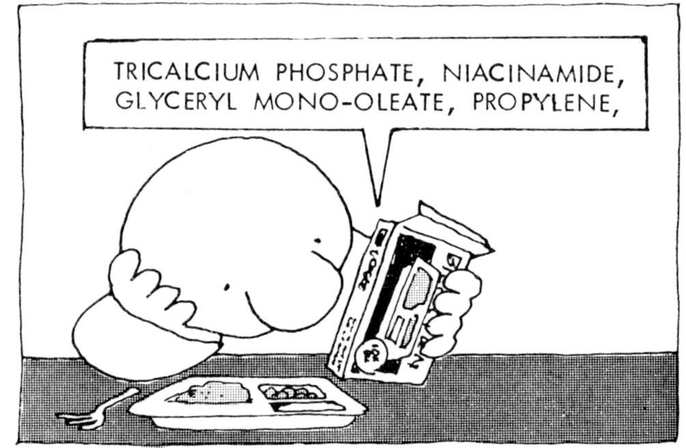
TRICALCIUM PHOSPHATE, NIACINAMIDE, GLYCERYL MONO-OLEATE, PROPYLENE,

. . ARTIFICIAL FLAVOUR, BHA AND BHT TO PREVENT SPOILAGE . . .

MY COMPLIMENTS TO THE CHEMIST !!

YOUR LUGGAGE IS OKAY...
...BUT YOU'RE OVERWEIGHT !!

UPCREEK AIRLINE

TOM WILSON

...IT MAY BE TRUE THAT THE HUMAN BODY IS THE TEMPLE OF OUR SOUL,....
...BUT YOU'VE BEEN GIVING YOURS TOO MANY BURNT OFFERINGS !!
Tom Wilson

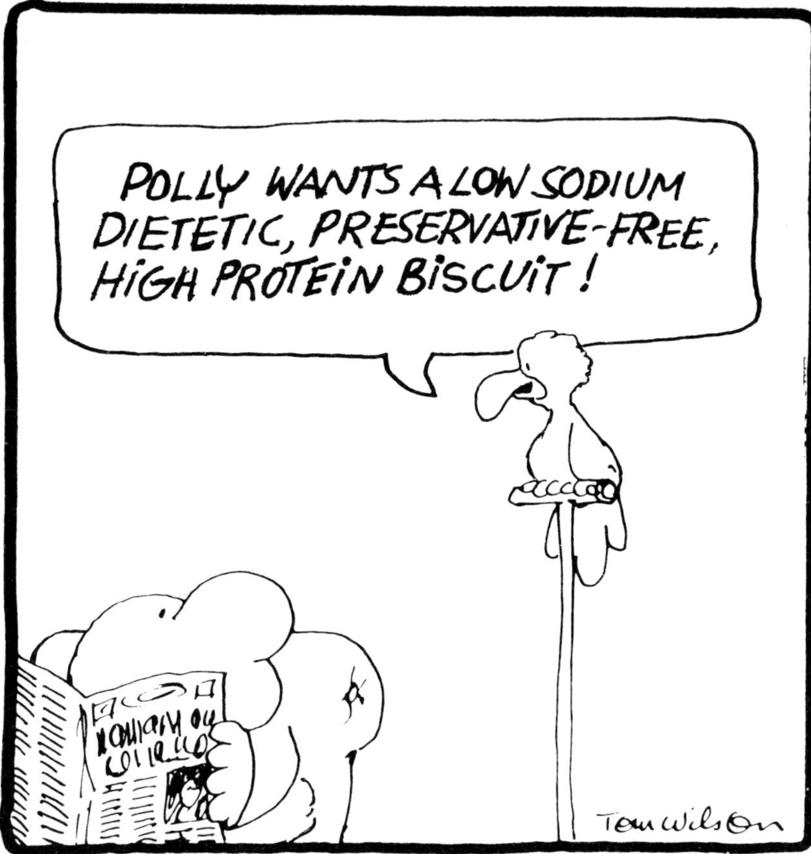
POLLY WANTS A LOW SODIUM DIETETIC, PRESERVATIVE-FREE, HIGH PROTEIN BISCUIT!
Tom Wilson

MUM'S
SNACK
BA
...THERE'S NO SALT CELLAR BECAUSE TOO MUCH SALT ISN'T GOOD FOR YOU!!
TOM WILSON

YOUR WEIGHT
AND A LIST OF FAMOUS FAT PEOPLE
10p

YOUR WEIGHT AND A TELLING OFF
10p
Tom Wilson

MY NAME iS AMRAC... i AM FROM THE PLANET SERUNAB.. ..AND YOU ARE STANDiNG ON MY FEET !!

YOUR WEIGHT and FORTUNE

You made a pig of yourself over the holidays ...which leaves you with one of two choices for the future:

1. Either lose 35 pounds

OR

2. Grow 18 inches taller

GOOD LUCK!

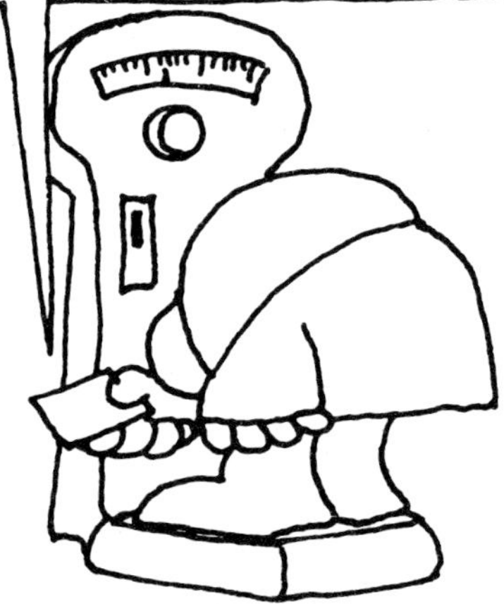

YOUR WEIGHT AND FORTUNE
YOU ARE 23 POUNDS OVERWEIGHT AND WILL MARRY A TALL DARK STRANGER BUT SACRIFICE YOUR CHANCE TO BECOME MISS UNITED KINGDOM

..YOU ARE THE PERFECT WEIGHT FOR A 7FT. 4 INCH MAN !!

..YOU ARE 20 POUNDS OVERWEIGHT, AND IT'S ALL YOUR FAULT !!
TOM WILSON

i WiSH THe HONeST WeiGHT WASN'T QUiTe SO HONeST....
HONEST WEiGHT
10p

FOR A HEALTHIER TOMORROW ..HEALTH FOODS !!
CLOSED DUE TO iLLNESS
Macguire's HEALTH FOODS

..I'M REALLY GLAD PEOPLE ARE BECOMING MORE CONCERNED ABOUT HEALTH, AND NUTRITION..
MO'S
Health Foods
DEFLOWERED FLOUR
YES WE HAVE LEAF MOULD
Vitamins A to Z

AHHH... AN OASIS IN THE MIDST OF THIS NUTRITIONLESS WAISTLAND!!
MO'S
Health Foods
DEFLOWERED FLOUR
YES WE HAVE LEAF MOULD
Vitamins A to Z

..I NEVER REALIZED HOW POOR MY DIET WAS TILL I STARTED READING UP ON NUTRITION, AND VITAMINS. AND STUFF !!!
MULCH
POWDERED LIVER
DEFLOWERED FLOUR
INSTANT GERM OF WHEAT

..IF A PERSON TAKES CARE OF HIS NUTRITIONAL NEEDS, HE CAN LIVE A LONG, AND HEALTHY LIFE !!
MO's
Health Foods
YES WE HAVE LEAF MOULD
Vitamins A to Z

"...IF YOU TAKE CARE OF YOUR BODY, YOUR BODY WILL TAKE CARE OF YOU."...

CARROT TOPS
BEAN SPROUTS
LEAF MOULD
TomWilson

• WARNING •
EXCESSIVE LABEL-READING COULD BE HARMFUL TO YOUR PEACE OF MIND !!

...i ONLY CAME iN TO BUY A DIET MEAL
SUPER SNAX

THE MOON REMINDS ME OF A BIG CHOCOLATE CREAM BICCY
...BUT THEN, EVERYTHING DOES!

..HOW'S THIS FOR A BALANCED DIET?!
GOOD HUMOUR

EMERGENCY WARD

Hugo's
HEALTH
FOODS
RING BELL
FOR
SERVICE

BAKERY
I'M A
FOOD VOYEUR

...IF YOU DON'T CONCENTRATE ON JAM DOUGHNUTS, THEY'LL GET YOU EVERY TIME!!

THIS DIET WILL BE A LOT EASIER TO FOLLOW IF YOU THINK OF YOURSELF AS A BUNNY RABBIT !

Tom Wilson

THERE..NOW THEY WON'T BE SITTING AROUND TEMPTING ME !!
BISCUITS
CHOC CHIP
Milk

Other gift books from Exley Publications

Ziggy: Plants are some of my favourite people, £2.95. This is a popular book of Ziggy cartoons. Ziggy is a born loser and his endearing failures make him appeal to all ages.
Ziggy and his plant have a very special relationship. His plant reacts emotionally, complains a great deal, gets depressed a lot, is jealous of the attention Ziggy gives any of his annuals and hates being left alone. A must for anyone who is potty about plants – or about Ziggy.
Ziggy: Pets are friends who share your rainy days, £2.95. Ziggy's pets are very special little people who run his life for him. Anyone who has loved a pet will see themselves in this book.
Ziggy: Work is a lousy way to earn a living, £2.50. A consolation book from Ziggy for all those mortals who trudge to work in the morning. How Ziggy copes (or fails to!) with inflation, his boss, the tax man and the rueful business of making ends meet. An attractive, low cost little hardback.
Ziggy: Know how much I love you, £1.95. This must be one of the smallest 'books' on sale: just 2¼ x 2¼ x 1 inch; yet the surprise concertina fold-out message extends to nearly five feet in length. Packed in a pretty heart-covered slip case this is a magic, zany little book that says it all. Children, mums, dads, lovers, grandads – everyone would love it on a special occasion.
Ziggy: Happy birthday to you . . ., £1.95. Another concertina message book nearly five feet in length to celebrate that special birthday. 2¼ x 2¼ x 1 inch, packed in its own slip case.

Simply order through your bookshop, or by post from Exley Publications Ltd, Dept ZD, 16 Chalk Hill, Watford, Herts, WD1 4BN. Please add 15p in the £ as a contribution to postage and packing.